Say Goodbye to the Pain of the Past:

For Men

Say Goodbye to the Pain of the Past:

For Men

Nadia Atkinson

Be You Nique Publishing

Say Goodbye to The Pain of The Past: For Men
By Nadia Atkinson
Published by Be You Nique Publishing
www.beyoutimes2.com

Cover art work by Janelle Jones
Editing by Kevin Howell for On Point Editing
Copyright © 2015
by Nadia Atkinson
All rights reserved.
Printed in the United States of America

DEDICATION

Realistically, you exist in my head but I haven't found you yet. The happiness you bring is like me sitting on the beach on a hot, sunny day. You'd understand how happy I am because you know how much I love the sand. You'd know that I am in love with you because I love the way the sunrays give me a tan. I'd know you're in love with me because you hate the sand, but you love how happy I am when you're there. My smile is everything to you. The way you stare at me to admire my beauty, and how I become shy and blush then cock my head to the side with a big grin – you give me a feeling that I can't explain. Our conversation is always deep and sensual, a meeting of the minds that no one can understand. You get me and I get you. Late nights watching shows about our universe and how amazing our God is. You, constantly covering me as wife, helper, and silent leader; Me, constantly praying for your protection as you go out into a world where you may feel inferior to man, trying to prove that you are greater than, yet doing it all in favor of me and our son-to-be. Our love is inseparable. Our love is undeniable. Our love is one with the Creator. Our love is literally a match made in heaven. The story has yet to be written on Earth, but it has been completed in Heaven. I love you and you love me, together we will write the story of WE. So until we meet, its words we cannot speak. Just know I will continue to pray for the day that we meet. This book is dedicated to you, my husband, whomever you may be.

TABLE OF CONTENTS

PREFACE XIII

A LETTER FOR YOU XVII

REDEEMED FROM THE LAW;

NOW DWELLING IN GRACE. 1

BEING ONE WITH GOD 11

LOST AND FOUND 19

MAN'S WILL; FREE WILL; GOD'S

WILL. 27

HOLDING ONTO GOD'S VISION 35

FROM A MALE TO A MAN 45

WHEN I THOUGHT I WAS ALONE –

THAT WAS WHEN GOD WAS THE

CLOSEST 61

MR. TRANSFORMED 83

MEN MADE BY MERCY 93

ACKNOWLEDGEMENTS

First and foremost, I give all praises to my Father in Heaven for blessing me with the vision for my second book, this book. It has certainly been a long journey with this title. I do not know when and how I would've finished this book if it weren't for Him. From all of the outside temptations to all of the distractions, to the many days and nights I neglected the words that flowed because I wasn't ready to pen them, God's timing is always, always, always perfect. Only He could have known that the temptations, distractions, and neglect would hinder me from writing this book for almost a year, yet He knew on one cold March day that I would sit down and just write for hours. He knew when the finished product was delivered it would be ready because He said so. Once again, His timing is perfect. There is no God like Jehovah. For this very reason, I will always serve Him. I love you. You saved me, you continue to save me and trust me to share your word in a way that I can only deliver it. Thank you for trusting me with such a task, and I am honored you chose me. Thank you for everything yesterday, today, and tomorrow.

Thank you to my parents for their continuous support and prayers: Dad, Mom, and Tasha, I love you. To my baby sis who is spreading her entrepreneurial wings, I love you to the moon and back. I always enjoy our conversations and can only pray we grow closer in our adult years. To my dear friends – my besties and family who always encourage me to go out and be great in Jesus' name – Twana, Christy, Shawana, Kanisha, Gina, Talisha, Lea, Chrissy, Ishela, Deronise, Robbie, Samantha, and Kris Cruz, your calls, texts, Facebook posts, likes, and shares are so greatly appreciated. You all keep me going and have a special place in my heart.

To my Kickstarter campaign backers: I don't want to single you out, I know some of you don't like that type of attention, but I am truly blessed and thankful for your support and faith in me and my talent. I bless you, I thank you, and this book wouldn't exist without you.

To the men and women who participated in this book, I thank you for your transparency and bravery for doing this project. I know some of this wasn't easy, and at times you may not have wanted to do it at all. I am glad you did and trusted me enough to share your shortcomings and victories with the world. Thank you.

Last but not least, I want to thank all of my Facebook friends and followers for all of your support. This past year was extremely difficult for me. I am not sure how I even got here in 2015, but I want to say thank you for your messages and support. You never missed a beat. When I knew this book was out of sight and mind, one of you would ask how it was going, and sometimes I was honest and other times I ignored you until I was ready to be honest. Thank you for that push, you have no clue how much it got me to this point. I am forever grateful. Peace and blessings to you.

PREFACE

Keep a cool head. Stay alert. The devil is poised to pounce and would like nothing better than to catch you napping. Keep your guard up. You're not the only one plunged into these hard times. It's the same with Christians all over the world. So keep a firm grip on the faith. The suffering won't last forever (1 Peter 5:8, 9 MSG). When I read this verse, it reminds me of the strength of a man. Although there is someone constantly wishing that you would fail, there is someone greater who wants the best for you, so you keep pushing forward.

This book, *Say Goodbye to The Pain of The Past: For Men*, was inspired by the many men who are pouring their hearts out to me weekly, if not daily, about their daily pressures. I thought about the first book I wrote and figured it would be a great idea to do the same for men. I didn't realize how difficult it would be to get information out of men, not realizing most men don't communicate in the same fashion as women. Clearly, women express themselves in much more detail than men do. I didn't realize this would be difficult for me until the interviews were already conducted and I had already announced the launch of a second book. I continued to pray and I continued to rely on the wisdom of God to get me through this process. I did not think I would ever finish this book because I was hearing so many negative things about it. The number one issue – I wasn't a man. Then I figured: Why would God give me this book to write if He didn't think I was capable of doing so? Being a man is a fraction of the issue. I have read many books for women written by men, plus I was merely shedding light on their past life, not giving advice on being a man. I could do this. That is what I did… this.

I pray that this book brings hope as it is my life's mission to do that: bring hope to the lost, bring light to a dark place, to open the eyes of those who don't think a way out is possible. I wrote this book for one to see that YOU ARE NOT ALONE. I felt alone many times and literally thought no one was there for me, and then I met the Christ. I would never force religion on anyone, but I would like for you to be open to knowledge. They say knowledge is power. How can one have a decent, structured conversation without knowledge? It is better to know than to fear the unknown. Take this book and read it to obtain knowledge and then decide if Jesus the Christ is for you. If he isn't then at least you are aware of the nine men who were blessed by his sacrifice some 2000-plus years ago. If he is for you, then I welcome you into the kingdom and know that the opening scripture of this preface is in fact something you will encounter daily. There is someone who hates God and wants to be just like him. In fact, he's a god, just in a darker world. The devil doesn't hate you, he just hates the fact you worship the one he doesn't; you are the middle man and he desires to hurt God because he knows God cares for you. I try to remember that when I am going through a trial because the devil wants nothing more than to see me curse the name of the Lord. I refuse; he has done too much for me to not be grateful. I pray this book opens your eyes to evil and you know that God is always here to save. Amen.

A LETTER FOR YOU
Man of God

"My aim is to know him, to experience the power of his resurrection, to share in his sufferings, and to be like him in his death…"
Phil 3:10 (NET Bible)

My brother, every day the media is plaguing our society with images of what a man should be and act like. From the screens on our movie theaters to the sports arena, they are distorted views and most of all, a lie! Many of these men are without character and insight, dishonorable in their business relations and marriages, arrogant and deceitful, lack self-control, lovers of themselves, and abusers of women and themselves, etc. This all stems from a world that does not yet know the Savior. Sadly, many of our men in the faith are imitating these behaviors because they do not know who they are in Christ.

My brother, aim to know our Savior's heart. He's the embodiment of what a man should be like. In your daily fellowship with Jesus, you will see and experience great changes in your life just because your desire is to know Him. Your life transformation will encourage many men to seek the real truth about what a real man is.

Finally, those daily temptations of life that try to make you stumble and feel condemnation and self-doubt, say with great boldness: "You have no power over me. I am strong in the power of His resurrection. I am FREE!" You are a mighty man of valor.

****

This letter is from a young lady who gave her testimony in *The Past is in the Past so Let it Pass: For Women*. You can read her testimony on "Finding True Love" on page 23 of the book.

Redeemed From the Law;

Now Dwelling in Grace.

Age: 36

Driver/Forklift Operator

"In him we have redemption through his blood, the forgiveness of sins, in accordance with the riches of God's grace."

(Ephesians 1:7 NIV)

Tell me what was your life like before Christ?

Before Christ, my life was a pure mess. I was in and out of trouble with the law from the age of 15 until I was 22 years old. I used to curse a lot. I used to hang out on the streets, sell drugs, and hang out with corrupt people. I didn't care too much about the people who were around me unless they were in my circle. I used to drink, smoke weed, and hang out on the corner. I thought that was the life. I thought doing this would make me look like a gangster, tough, someone not to be messed with. After I gave my life to Christ, one of the first things I stopped doing was cursing. The things I used to do as far as hanging out on the streets and cursing people out, I stopped that. This was something that God truly did for me, he gave me a complete makeover. I am no longer afraid and I am going to church. I am saved and a born-again Christian. I have been saved for 15 years now. I thank God each and every day that I wake up. He kept my mind sane. I could be dead and gone, sleeping in my grave, but because of who God is and who he is in my life, I am alive and well today.

What does your salvation mean to you?

Salvation means the world to me. When I first told people I gave my life to Christ, I was 21 and they said I wouldn't be saved that long because I was on the corner selling drugs, drinking, and smoking. But look at me now! Fifteen years later and I am still saved and still standing on his word. If he can keep me, he can definitely keep anybody. Just knowing that Jesus died on the cross for my sins lets me know that when this life is over, I will reign with him in Heaven.

If you could save someone by telling them one thing God has done for you in your life, what would it be?

God has done so many things for me it would literally take a whole lifetime to tell you. If I had to think of one thing specifically, it would be when I was 20 years old and I was already in trouble with the law in New York, so I decided to take some drugs to sell with me to North Carolina. I got busted with the drugs in the state of Virginia. I was facing 20 years in prison for the amount of drugs I had and also for transporting them. It amounted to 10 years for transporting and another 10 years for the amount of drugs. Again, I was only 20 years old at the time. I had a court date for January 7, 1999, and God showed up and showed out for me. The court did not know that I had a record from New York, so instead of them giving me 20 years in prison, they only made me do 10½ months in the Virginia jail. That was truly a lifesaver within itself.

Describe some of the daily pressures you have to face as a godly man and how do you overcome them?

Some of the daily pressures I face is trusting and believing in God when the bills come in and having faith to know that God will provide.

Tell me why you couldn't imagine your life without God.

If it wasn't for the Lord who was on my side I really don't know where I would be today.

Men have a lot to live up to in the Bible as husbands according to Ephesians 5:21-33. Is it difficult to live up to these standards now as a husband or when you decide to marry? Why?

It is not difficult because of the simple fact that I am saved. Everything I do I try to direct it toward Christ. I try to live my life according to what the Bible says I am supposed to be. Everything I do I put God first. Is this something Christ would want me to do? Is this something that would bring glory and honor to

4

God? By me saying this, I always have to check myself to make sure it is something that lines up with the word. I don't think it is hard because I read the word and I understand a lot of what the Bible tells me, especially about what a man is supposed to be. A man is supposed to work; the Bible says if a man doesn't work, he doesn't eat. Therefore, I know a man is not supposed to be lazy being a man. You have to take care of the responsibilities of being the head of your household. By you being the head, you have to go out and labor. You have to lead by example. You can't just stay at home and tell your wife to work. I have to go out and show that I am a man and that I can go out and provide for my family. This shows that by me going to church and praising God and showing them that it is alright, it shows that I am a man first, and although God is invisible, he is everything to me. Without him, I am nothing. I am not ashamed to let anyone know that he is everything to me. He opened doors that seemed closed to me before. It is not hard to be a godly husband and following after Christ because Christ laid the example when he went out and witnessed. It is not difficult at all as

5

long as you read your word and submit to Christ. That is the number one thing: If you submit to Christ, He will be able to dictate exactly what your life is supposed to be. The Bible says if God be for us, who can be against? I believe that as long as I have the Lord on my side, he will give me the strength and wisdom to get through any situation that may arise in my life.

If you could describe your relationship with God, what would you say about it? How does it help you day to day?

I seek God first, I put him first, I can't even brush my teeth without God. I literally mean that. I can't do that without his presence. I can't take credit for waking up. If God does not literally touch me to wake me up in the morning – there is no alarm clock, He touches me to wake me up. I could be somewhere eating straw, not knowing where I am. He kept my mind; He keeps my mind. He gives me a peace that surpasses all understanding. I am so grateful for anything and everything he has done for me. I can't take any credit for anything – my marriage, the car I drive, everything that I have. I am in awe of everything that he is doing in my life. I look forward to going to church on Sunday, going to Bible study on Wednesday, and just being able to read the word. My relationship with God is everything to me. I pray every day just to say thank you for the small things like the fact that no one hits my car when I am on the road driving; thank you for keeping me safe at work. I thank him for patience to deal with my infant daughter when I am tired. I pray to him and I thank him. I am not ashamed of that. I love Him. He is the head of my life. I can do nothing. I literally can't brush my teeth or stand if he does not give me the strength. It is only God who allows me to be able to continue to walk this walk. Who am I for him to allow me to be able to sit here to give this interview? My relationship with Him is like no other. I put him first and everything else comes second. My relationship with God is very special. He is my everything.

Tell me, what is the most valuable lesson you have learned summed up in one sentence?

"Greater is He that is with me than he that is in the world."

This testimony repeats the words kept me, keep me, keeps me. What does this mean exactly? It means God will literally continue to bestow his blessings upon you. He will continue to hold you in his arms even though it may feel like he is barely holding on by a fingertip. He will provide for you all that you have been lacking as long as you remember him, believe in him, and know he is real.

This gentleman was exposed to a very dangerous lifestyle most wouldn't dare to enter. He struggled with identity, which many of us can relate to. We desire to be things we know we are not supposed to be. In this case, he was a drug dealer who dodged many bullets because God had greater for his life. As a husband, he is aware that life does not revolve around him. He knows that without God his liabilities wouldn't be paid, his home wouldn't have peace, and he wouldn't have peace without the grace of God. No one can and will ever say that God hasn't allowed him to survive, dodge, miss, or escape some major event that has happened in his life that he would have never gotten out of if it weren't for "something." That something is God.

The one thing that humbled me while listening to this testimony was the fact that he said: "There is no alarm clock, God touches me and wakes me up daily!" That moment you wake up to your alarm going off some may think: "Here we go again, another day, another dollar"; "Why is this baby crying now?"; "Why is it so cold in this house?"; "Why is it so hot in this house?"; "Why is this woman annoying me so early in the morning?" There are so many other first thoughts when it comes to waking up in the morning. I too am guilty of not always thanking God for waking me up because I prefer to sleep until the last minute before I have to get ready for work, then I am rushing for my life to get out of the door on time. REM (rapid eye movement) sleep is a calm, peaceful, and dreamlike state of sleeping. It allows our muscles to become paralyzed, and we are engulfed in a dream state. When I think of death, I can easily think about REM sleep and how we are not conscious of our thoughts until we move back into the first stage of sleeping. God can easily transition us from sleeping in a "light" sleep to an eternal sleep, but every morning for the past however many days we have been living, he wakes us up to start a new day. He allows us to have another day where we can go out and make a difference, be great, do great, and get one step closer to what our purpose is here on this Earth. We cannot let Him down. We must not let Him down. As a man, you will not let Him down. You were made to lead, guide, build, and protect. Everyone and everything in life depends on you. Society looks up to you. Other men, women, and children look up to you. You have to be bold and be this person you never intended to be. That person is easy to become with the help of the Lord.

Being One With God

Age: 33

Youth Pastor

[8] Not only those things; I reckon everything as complete loss for the sake of what is so much more valuable, the knowledge of Christ Jesus my Lord. For his sake I have thrown everything away; I consider it all as mere garbage, so that I may gain Christ [9] and be completely united with him. I no longer have a righteousness of my own, the kind that is gained by obeying the Law. I now have the righteousness that is given through faith in Christ, the righteousness that comes from God and is based on faith.

(Philippians 3:8-9 GNT)

Tell me what was your life like before Christ?

My life was like anyone else who would live without God – clubbing, hanging out with the boys, doing all types of things that most people do. I always went to church but I really wasn't saved. I had put on a facade as if I was, but really was not. I was in church Sunday morning then in the club Sunday night. One incident I recall God saving me was just some years ago after my divorce. I was in a stage of depression; I did not realize what I was getting myself into. I was stepping more away from God than to him. On one particular day, I decided to take a drive with a female friend and my two kids. On my way back home, we were in the highway and a chair was right in front of us. I tried to avoid it and caused the vehicle I was driving to flip three times into the woods off the freeway. This was a wake-up call for me seeing that not one of us was hurt, not even a scratch, but the vehicle was totaled. God had his hands on me that day and I realized I was in disobedience and certain people needed to be cut off from my life.

What does your salvation mean to you?

My salvation means that God really loves me for who I am. God took his only son's life and gave it up for me. He salvaged my life and turned it into something much greater than I have ever expected.

If you could save someone by telling them one thing God has done for you in your life, what would it be?

I would have to say that one thing would be when he kept me when I was homeless. I slept in my car for months and no one knew. So if I can at least help save someone from making the wrong choice of not accepting God, it would be to let them know that God is truly real. He kept me safe even in the midst of me being homeless. And the only thing that really kept me from not going insane was when I was listening to worship music. It really helped me to call on God more and really pray.

Describe some of the daily pressures you have to face as a godly man and how do you overcome them?

Daily pressures as a man can be a very long list. I have the pressure of being a single father and really learning how to be a godly father. Also the pressures of women trying to tempt you, whether you're married or not, can be enough to break one within itself. But overcoming them is not a hard thing to do. When you're so saturated in the things of God, you learn how to trust even with the smallest things. So it's overcome by prayer and guidance by the Holy Spirit. You do this by first having an intimate relationship with Christ. Christ told his disciples that he was sending a comforter in John 14:16; we should always be willing to yield to the Spirit of God. This only becomes harder if we do not kill our flesh on a daily basis.

Tell me why you couldn't imagine your life without God.

Life without God is like a car without an engine. He starts my day that allows me to breath, walk, talk, etc. God is the engine that keeps me going. Everything I am and have become is because of God. The person I once was was arrogant, prideful, and just plain lost – the one who seems to have it all together but has nothing. From the outside, it looks real good, but inside I was really hurting, trying to create this false reality within myself. To add to all the mayhem, as everything became worse, the better I tried to look. It made no sense. That is something I never want to go back to. Even though I went to church, God was not evident in my life. I shut him out; I ignored his word. I was looking at others in the church who were doing the opposite of the word of God and thought I could do the same, and the more I did the opposite of God, the more he allowed me to dig my way down until I really wanted God for myself. The man I once was in the clubs, being homeless, and a sexual deviant was all just me not knowing who I was in Christ.

Men have a lot to live up to in the Bible as husbands according to Ephesians 5:21-33. Is it difficult to live up to these standards now as a husband or when you decide to marry? Why?

My answer to that is no! Nothing is hard if you really sit down and think about it. Things may become challenging, even nerve-wracking sometimes, but not hard. Being a husband is a privilege because God gave the wife as a gift. Whenever you have a gift that you really wanted, you do everything possible to protect it, cherish it, and preserve it. But you will only do this once you understand who you are as a man of God and what God has placed in your hands.

If you could describe your relationship with God, what would you say about it? How does it help you day to day?

My relationship with God is an intimate one. Once again, you do this by first having an intimate relationship with Christ. Christ told his disciples that he was sending a comforter in John 14:16; we should always be willing to yield to the spirit of God. This only becomes harder if we do not kill our flesh on a daily basis. Since I'm a worship leader and youth pastor, I have learned the importance of intimacy with the Father. It helps me to be much more transparent as I am being now. Daily I trust him with my life!

Tell me, what is the most valuable lesson you have learned summed up in one sentence?

That greater is HE than he who is in the world!

****

Oftentimes we hear people say that prior to drawing closer to God, their lives were a mess or full of chaos and they had no sense of direction. Now they have this amazing life they could have never imagined. Just think about it: Imagine this man, his friend, and two children in a car driving down a highway. There is a chair in the middle of a highway, the car flips, and everyone in the car is perfectly fine, but the car is totaled. God put Jesus on this Earth and placed a cross in the middle of him and heaven, similar road but in order for him to get down that road he had no choice but to hit that cross in order to sit on the right hand of our Father in Heaven. (After the Lord Jesus had spoken to them, he was taken up into heaven and he sat at the right hand of God. – Mark 16:19 NIV) Jesus' bones were not broken (These things happened so that the scripture would be fulfilled: "Not one of his bones will be broken," John 19:36 NIV), not one single bone was broken. The people inside the car, their bones were not harmed or broken. It is impossible not to give God the glory for being alive after surviving a horrific car crash as this young man did. This one incident allowed him to dedicate his life to God for good. God kept him safe from harm when he was homeless. God protects his mind and increases him with wisdom when raising his children. God shields him from lusting over women who tempt him. I am sure if we asked him how many things God has protected him from or continues to protect him from, there would be a longer list. God is worthy of all praise. What is God to you?

Lost and Found

Age: 30

Electrician

"[28] And we know that all things work togeth er for good to those who love God, to those who are the called according to *His* purpos e. [29] For whom He foreknew, He also prede stined *to be* conformed to the image of His Son, that He might be the firstborn among many brethren."

(Romans 8:28, 29 NKJV)

Tell me what was your life like before Christ?

My life before Christ was full of uncertainty and what-ifs. I lived a reckless life full of dead ends, sometimes suicidal thoughts because of the pressure I put on myself to live up to people's expectations they had for me. At times, the emptiness that I had in my life that I tried to fill with alcohol, drugs, and being promiscuous day after day wasn't enough; my

19

problems kept escalating. I got two DUIs back to back and I know that those actions allowed God to accept me and bring me back closer to Him. I'm so thankful He did. I live my life on purpose for a purpose now. I no longer stress over man's failures or letdowns. I keep my faith and I always know the impossible is possible through Christ.

The drugs that I took were marijuana and of course alcohol. The marijuana had a control over me as if I needed it, then I started thinking I'm better with it. I would smoke before work because of the depression I was going through with the DUIs. The stress of the court cases, the money I didn't have to pay for a lawyer, and the fact that I really had no one in my corner to help me get through this difficult time really hurt. That's when the suicidal thoughts started to enter my mind. I wondered who would miss me if I was gone. I cried one night because I had to write out my thoughts. It made me realize I would be missed by all of my loved ones. It turned out that I do have a lot of people who care about me. Unfortunately, my support system lived in New Jersey and I was in Georgia.

The club scene made me feel good. The music and the alcohol made me feel as if nothing was wrong, but it just put me in a deeper state of depression that was written all over my face. Overall, the DUIs cost me about $17,000 – $13,000 for the lawyer, $3,000 in fines plus the hours missed from work, and the DUI school. I've lost a lot, but I've gained so much. I needed to be in that dark place so God could open my eyes to see that He was what I needed. Suicide was never the answer. There's no need to quit when God has your back.

What does your salvation mean to you?

My salvation to me is my rebirth. I was born July 1984 and was born again on February 24, 2013. Rebirth to me means a second chance at life with a purpose. God gave me a second chance to live my life without fear of the unknown. Doors opened up for me that I thought were closed. The ability to pray with confidence knowing my prayers will be answered.

If you could save someone by telling them one thing God has done for you in your life, what would it be?

God's work speaks for itself. People can see the improvement in my life and how I've become a better man. Job opportunities have opened up for me. I use less profanity when I speak. I'm actively involved in church. I no longer wake up ready to get the day over with; I wake up now with a sense of purpose because you never know whose life you might touch.

Describe some of the daily pressures you have to face as a godly man and how do you overcome them?

The people that I hang out with do not live by faith, they are still trapped in the world of committing sins. Every so often I feel the need to give into it because they are my friends and that's what I used to do. But God has a way of pulling me back! He knows how to reach me. What I mean by give into the pressures is I put myself back in bad situations such as going out and getting drunk, doing drugs, and being promiscuous. I know that's all my friends seem to think about; however, they have good intentions and that's all the life they know because they are used to it. I say a prayer and ask God to guide me back to Him to keep me safe away from my old lifestyle.

Tell me why you couldn't imagine your life without God.

I can't imagine my life without God because I remember life before him and it was scary. I would never want to go back to that. His love and the love he has for me is real.

Men have a lot to live up to in the Bible as husbands according to Ephesians 5:21-33. Is it difficult to live up to these standards now as a husband or when you decide to marry? Why?

It's only difficult if you allow outside distractions to influence your thinking of how a husband should be. The most important factor to me in the Bible is, "Husbands love your wives just as Christ loves the church, give yourself up for her." That speaks volumes to me as a husband. In my opinion, if you're not right with God, how can you set up a good foundation for the house? A home isn't a home unless you have God in it.

If you could describe your relationship with God, what would you say about it? How does it help you day to day?

My relationship with God is amazing. A week ago I prayed for his guidance through this financial burden I've been going through, and the next day I was offered a job with unlimited overtime. I have a monthly budget written out that I put in my Bible and no matter what, I always make it. I smile because I know no matter what God is working on it is always in my favor.

Tell me, what is the most valuable lesson you have learned summed up in one sentence?

"Trust in the Lord with all your heart and lean not on your own understanding; in all ways acknowledge him and he will make straight your paths." – Proverbs 3:5-6

****

I remember one particular year I was turning 23 and I never partied for my 21st birthday and wanted to get a little crazy. That is what I did. I literally did some crazy things that entire birthday weekend. I started on a Friday night after work and by Sunday I was walking barefoot around New York City completely drunk looking for my car at 4:30 in the morning. Thank God I had a bunch of my friends and family around me who guided me and protected me that evening. I am sure I would have never made it home if I was alone. At some point during that night I blacked out because I mixed Grey Goose Vodka with Moet Champagne. It was my birthday and my friend bought me a bottle of Champagne at the night club I was celebrating at. Who knew having a glass of Moet in one hand and a glass of Grey Goose in another would result in bare feet, a spinning room, and lots of lost memories the next morning. Although I believe it was a fun night for most, I remembered worrying about how people felt or if they had a good time once I woke up. That was my only concern.

We often seek validation from people, and many times our peers. The desire to fit in is always something that one struggles with. It is never OK to be in a circle alone, if you decided to be alone all of the time you're either depressed or lonely. Two scriptures come to mind when I think about pleasing man rather than God: John 12:43 (ESV) – "For they loved the glory that comes from man more than the glory that comes from God," and Galatians 1:10 (ESV) – "For am I now seeking the approval of man, or of God? Or am I trying to please man? If I were still trying to please man, I would not be a servant of Christ." You cannot please both God and man. Our God is a jealous God (Exodus 34:14). He is not one to accept second place when He gives us life daily. He gives and gives some more. He is the reason why grace is constant. The definition of constant is a situation or state of affairs that does not change. Another definition is unchangingly faithful and dependable. I don't know about you, but God has been extremely faithful to me even when I can't say the same about myself. No matter what, He stays close and doesn't allow me to stray too far off the path. He has mapped out our future and walks before us to keep us on that path and makes it straight. He is Alpha and Omega, Beginning and the End. He knows you better than anyone else. How and why would you allow someone or something to be before Him?

Man's Will; Free Will; God's Will.

Age: 21

Entrepreneur and Division 1 College Football player

"And it shall come to pass
That whoever calls on the name of the
LORD
Shall be saved."

(Acts 2:21 NKJV)

Tell me what was your life like before Christ?

It wasn't out of the ordinary. I did party a lot more and used a more urban vocabulary, but then God showed me my purpose on this Earth and I eliminated that as well as a few people out of my life. My vocabulary has definitely changed, it became more diverse in a positive way.

What does your salvation mean to you?

It means that you will have eternal life and will go to heaven with our Father.

If you could save someone by telling him or her one thing God has done for you in your life, what would it be?

He showed me that he has a purpose for everybody on this Earth. He also showed me it's not about how much money you have but the influence you have on people around you in a positive way. Rich is a mind-set, it's not monetary.

Describe some of the daily pressures you have to face as a godly man and how do you overcome them?

I try not to lose my composure when someone gets me upset. Sometimes it gets hard because I have a short temper, but then I remember our Father. God has expectations for all godly men that we must adhere to, and I don't want to slip up and not do as I'm supposed to.

Tell me why you couldn't imagine your life without God.

I don't know where I would be. Just being able to speak to him daily and him help me and guide me and nurture me, without that, I don't know what direction I would be moving in.

Men have a lot to live up to in the Bible as husbands according to Ephesians 5:21-33. Is it difficult to live up to these standards now as a husband or when you decide to marry? Why?

No it is not difficult to live up to these standards. It is not asking for anything out of the ordinary. I think once you have the mind-set of a man and not a little boy or child, you realize you have responsibilities and there are things that you must do as a man.

If you could describe your relationship with God, what would you say about it? How does it help you day to day?

My relationship with God is like no other relationship I have with anyone else. I feel like it has built me into the man I am today. He has bestowed an abundance of blessings on me spiritually, financially, mentally, and emotionally.

Tell me, what is the most valuable lesson you have learned summed up in one sentence?

Don't take life for granted.

******

Although he may be young in age, he has a very mature perspective on life. Oftentimes the pressure of being a man starts from toddler age. Boys are taught never to cry when they fall, to stand up and be a man because boys don't cry. They are told: protect your sister, fight back, be strong. Being a man starts early, and learning from another male figure helps, otherwise they are stuck learning from their mother. (No disrespect toward mothers, but a man can and should only learn to be a man from another man.) Many times this allows men to have a sensitive side and a softer side toward many situations in life. As we can see from this testimony, this young man was known for having a bad temper and he used his relationship with God to help him turn his anger into something else – a student-teacher relationship where he relies on God for growth.

We have the greatest lesson from David in Psalms where he freely spoke to God and relied on God's strength for growth. Psalm 18:2 says: "The LORD is my rock and my fortress and my deliverer, My God, my rock, in whom I take refuge; My shield and the horn of my salvation, my stronghold." God is our stronghold. He will deliver us from all pain and sorrow, and he will deliver us from ourselves. At times, we can be our own worst enemy. Our minds can encourage us to go left instead of right. We blame the devil for all wrongdoing when we forget that God has given us free will. What is free will? Free will is a choice or choices that are not predestined by God. We have a tendency to follow our human instinct or natural instinct instead of the spirit (the Holy Spirit) to guide us with our daily decisions. We often will make decisions and choices based on the desires of our flesh and our hearts, and in the Bible it mentions how sin begins with the desires of our hearts. James 1:13-15 sums this up quite nicely, it says:

¹³ When tempted, no one should say, "God is tempting me.
"For God cannot be tempted by evil, nor does he tempt
anyone;
¹⁴ but each person is tempted when they are dragged away by
their own evil desire and enticed.
¹⁵ Then, after desire has conceived, it gives birth to sin; and
sin, when it is full-grown, gives birth to death.

How many occasions can you think of where a thought repeats over and over and over again in your mind when you know it has already given birth to sin? When something is repeatedly reminding you of what your true heart's desire is, it is almost as good as done. We have to remember what Jesus' sacrifice was during those moments and in every moment when we feel sin creeping into our hearts. Let me paint a picture for you: I sit and watch these movies of Jesus' life, and we always see how badly beaten he was. I weep when I see it because, as an artist, my imagination travels extremely fast. One person can see what is physically happening, Jesus is being beaten, while I am looking at words being thrown on Jesus as he is being beaten, as if he is being beaten with the struggles we deal with daily. Words like hatred, molestation, cancer, depression, disease, hurt, heartbreak, and the list can go on for miles. But then I think about two more things – propitiation and defeating darkness. Imagine God's wrath – better yet, let's not. In the same way we believe that God is the master of impossible, I am quite certain we cannot fathom what his wrath would be like – that is impossible. Jesus saved us from that. If there was no hope of Satan's expiration date, how many people would actually follow God? Have you ever thought about that? If Jesus didn't die for our sins – past, present, and future – and if he didn't nail all of our sins to the cross, we wouldn't be able to have a hope for everlasting life. Jesus became what he hated THE MOST – **SIN** – so that we would be able to enjoy a perfect life one day (2 Corinthians 5:21). Jesus is the reason we can sleep at night knowing we probably sinned at some point during the day. He gives us hope. This is why it is so important to share the word of God with others. Little examples of you that reflect Jesus go a long way. This can eventually lead to someone's salvation. What greater gift can you give someone? There is none. Think about that.

Holding onto God's Vision

Age: 58

Managing Partner - Consulting Firm

Where there is no vision [no redemptive revelation of God], the people perish; but he who keeps the law [of God, which includes that of man]—blessed (happy, fortunate, and enviable) is he.

(Proverbs 29:18 AMP)

Tell me what was your life like before Christ?

My life as youth, teenager, and even young adult (college) was focused around three to four integral components: Christ, family, sports, community, and education. However, it was only in the latter part of my senior year of high school, where I was the top high school football player in the area, that I truly accepted Christ as my Lord and Savior. But prior to that, and even well into my junior year of

35

college, I was your typical young boy and teenager, and again, college student. In essence, that means experimenting and exploring, whether that be through challenging/questioning authority, involvement with girls/young ladies, and even the occasional smoking of weed in college. Whatever actions or steps I took that deviated from the norm of the road less traveled for which my parents had established and imprinted in my life, it was never "too" far. Although I hadn't accepted Christ as my Savior until my senior year of high school, the conviction of my "bad" actions were because I knew in my heart that my parents would not approve. So, truthfully speaking, they were my earthy example of the relationship between Christ and the church, and in hindsight, displeasing them was displeasing God.

What does your salvation mean to you?

Simply put, it is biblical optimism for me, meaning faith. The net of that is having a sincere and true heart to serve others with the belief and hope that others would come to know Jesus as the Christ. Although far from perfect, I sincerely hope that my life is an example of that, less my words, but my life. The old Baptist preachers used to often say, "It's better to see a good sermon than hear one."

If you could save someone by telling them one thing God has done for you in your life, what would it be?

I recently attended a ceremony that was paying tribute to a man who had passed away, but who poured into the lives of so many young folks over the decades. It was held in one of the surrounding communities in my old stomping grounds of New York where I spent my teenage and my college years.

This particular occasion brought together folks who hadn't seen one another in years, decades even, although many had connected via social media (e.g. Facebook, etc.). But it was a very surreal moment for me. Not only coming face to face with my past, but in some cases, seeing how hard life had been on so many that I grew up with and knowing that if it had not been for God's saving grace, perhaps someone would have been looking at me that day saying, "Oh my," as I found myself saying about others during that day's ceremony.

Describe some of the daily pressures you have to face as a godly man and how do you overcome them?

I believe too often men, especially those who are married and/or have a family, go day to day without a true vision for their lives individually, as a husband, and as a father. So that often they just wing it or find themselves reacting versus being proactive. Helen Keller was asked if blindness was the worse handicap. She responded by saying, "No, it's a man who has sight but no vision." Yes, as men we should be active in providing for our family, meaning putting food on the table, clothes on their back, and a roof over their head. But that's maintaining a family, or let me take it one step further, that's providing for the family. Even that is not the full context of provision. Provision equals pro & vision: pro meaning ahead/before/forward, and vision meaning able to see. You are called to see ahead for your marriage, for your children, and for your family! Hence, the idea of marriage and parental coalition is an awesome testimony of God's love. First and foremost, challenges and pressures are a part of life, but as someone once spoke over my life, I do my best to apply what was prophetically shared relative to my life, albeit I don't always hit the bull's-eye.

"And it will not come without challenge and test, but you shall rise to the

occasion, for you shall seek me.

"And you shall not slack in your prayer commitment, and you shall know

that it's not all work, but you will set aside time to be with Me, saith God."

Tell me why you couldn't imagine your life without God.

One word: emptiness.

Men have a lot to live up to in the Bible as husbands according to Ephesians 5:21-33. Is it difficult to live up to these standards now as a husband or when you decide to marry? Why?

Marriage is a covenant relationship between husband and wife, which represents God's earthly example of the relationship between Christ and the Church. Not only is there a spiritual attack on marriage, but families as a whole. And as we have seen from the beginning of time, with the enemy, along with our own selfishness, we can often find ourselves being challenged, and at times, compromising our moral and spiritual standards as husbands. Get rid of us (the husband) and the house will begin to fall, and it becomes a domino effect, often for generations to come.

If you could describe your relationship with God, what would you say about it? How does it help you day to day?

Honestly, it is revealing. The more I allow him to take complete control over *every* aspect of my life, the greater peace I have and the more I see the *me* he wants me to be versus the me that I often find myself looking at in the mirror. In order for me to allow Him to mold me, that goes back to one of my previous comments, which is biblical optimism equals faith.

Tell me, what is the most valuable lesson you have learned summed up in one sentence?

That the God I serve is a God of true mercy and grace.

Despite my flaws, my mistakes, and every other segment of me that "man" would judge me, turn away from me, and cast me out, my Lord lovingly corrects me, loves me, embellishes me, and encourages me almost simultaneously, which allows me to walk in peace despite how others may feel or think.

****

There were so many significant things that were said during this interview and only one stood out the most: "Get rid of us (the husband), and the house will begin to fall, and it becomes a domino effect often for generations to come." I pray that you understand how critical it is for you to be in your family's life. Whether that means for your partner or for your children, you have to be the example that many of our parents had when they were growing up in intact families (both parents in the home). Thirty-three percent of all children living in the United States are fatherless according to fathers.com. It appears to be a small number, but that 33 percent equates to 24.7 million children. That is huge! I honestly couldn't imagine my life without my dad in it. Growing up, he wasn't in the same home as I was due to my parents splitting when I was 6; however, I was able to maintain a relationship with him throughout the years. He was not an absentee parent; neither was my mom. I was still able to call on them when and if I needed them. Many children cannot. I think about so many examples of children in need of their parents – most importantly their fathers. For a young boy growing up without one, he could miss out on so many opportunities such as the impartiality and the consequences of right and wrong, healthy competition, understanding the boundaries in male-female relationships, receiving tough love, and how to love his wife like Christ loved the church, as mentioned in this testimony. For young girls, they need their dads to teach them how to boost their self-esteem and body image by showering them with love daily. Dads teach them how they ought to be loved and how to feel protected.

I think of Adam in Genesis 2 and how God was teaching him how to be a man before the woman came. He was placed in the Garden of Eden to tend and keep it. He named animals, he spent time with the Lord, and he followed the Lord's rules and requests. These are things God requires of men: to go to work and take care of their homes, procreate with their wives, and name their children. You spend time individually with the Lord so he can guide you and show you how to follow his rules and requests. It is the *same exact thing*. Why wouldn't we today need our fathers more than ever if Adam needed his father thousands of years ago? A father is vital to the growth of his child. Once that piece of the puzzle is missing, it is incomplete. You cannot look at the beautiful picture that is trying to be displayed if you are missing a piece.

From a Male to a Man

Age: 26

Bank
Teller/Entrepreneur/Minister/Musician

**"Blessed *is* the man
Who walks not in the counsel of the
ungodly,
Nor stands in the path of sinners,
Nor sits in the seat of the scornful;"**

(Psalms 1:1)

Tell me what was your life like before Christ?

I was raised in church all my life, but I went to church out of religious beliefs. My family went to church so I went to church. It wasn't until I was 16 when I had an encounter with God because my mother was diagnosed with stomach cancer. She was dying and I was watching her die. I went into my room once and I got angry with God because both my mom and my father were the perfect example of what Christian life is. They tried their hardest to live right, "Why is this happening?" It was right after she gave us her last words, so to speak, I went in the room and slammed the door and asked God, "Why?" I said, "If you are real, and you want everybody to serve you, heal my mother." Two weeks later I went to church and my pastor then was taking communion and told my mother to drink seven cups, and after the seventh cup she said she felt a lightning bolt hit her and she fell out. She went back to the doctor and did not have a trace of cancer. That sealed my beliefs.

After that, my life wasn't squeaky clean. I still wasn't ready to give God a complete yes. I was a musician in the church, and when you're a musician there are certain things that are attracted to you naturally, like women. I was exposed to sex at an early age because I was molested, so being in church was just church. I was into reckless things with churchgoers. There was debauchery and foolishness. I really didn't have respect for God because of what I saw. Outside of my parents, I saw church people talk about each other, married people sleeping with this one. I saw many people not having respect for church as an institution or God. I respected my parents but not church. After some time, I definitely did partake in some of the reckless activities with various women in the church. It was just a downward spiral from that.

I was always known as a church boy. My only weakness or downfall was women.

What does your salvation mean to you?

Wow. My salvation back then, I didn't really even know what it was because, coming from a religious background, you just thought to hell with your beliefs. You sin, you're going to hell. That was it. There was no remedy; it was legalistic. Now, coming to Faith Fellowship Ministries and hearing Pastor [David] Demola speak, it is kind of changing my mind now because this was instilled for years and years. Conviction, condemnation, and I was always taught that if you sin and you don't feel bad about it, you have a problem because you're always supposed to feel bad about it. Now that I am hearing his teaching, it is liberating because this whole time I was living a life of a lie basically. I felt like I had to live a certain

47

way to get closer to God. I had to fast and do religious things to get closer to Him. That is what my salvation was. My salvation back then was solely what I did and what I gave to God. If I didn't pray or if I didn't read, I didn't feel like I was saved. I wasn't a believer because I was trying to do it on my own by works and not faith.

Now, it is like a complete 360. I am an ordained minister, I've been in church my whole life, I am 26 years old, and I am just finding out what real foundation is and how Jesus actually did everything for me. I was stuck in the old way for so long and now I am trying to find the right way. It is amazing because every day I wake up and I am blown away. It makes so much more sense now than it did back then. Back then I felt like this can't be it, this doesn't make sense, and I could never explain why. But now, my salvation is my belief because He did everything for me. I just have to do my part.

If you could save someone by telling them one thing God has done for you in your life, what would it be?

God delivered me from people and their opinions. I always valued what people thought about me and I never valued what I thought about myself. I didn't even bother to imagine what God thought about me. I was always a people pleaser, and that led me to do things I did not really want to do, but because I didn't want to make anyone mad, I would do it. It basically got to a point where my relationship with God got put on the backburner because I was living for people and wasn't living for Him. See, my priorities were totally jacked up; at one point it was completely a stalemate in my life because my priorities were jacked up. When your priorities are jacked up, God cannot take you where your character cannot keep you. You can have the most potential in the world: as a singer I was anointed to sing, but I would never go anywhere because my priorities were messed up. My character wasn't right and as a result, nothing really happened. Then when God began to deal with me about how he has to be first, it kind of changed my whole outlook on life. It doesn't really matter because I realized that if I please God, nine times out of 10, I can please everybody else on the strength of allowing God to be my truth.

Describe some of the daily pressures you have to face as a godly man and how do you overcome them?

There is a difference between a man and a male. A man takes responsibility for everything he says he can't do, a male doesn't. Sad to say, but with the world's thinking, we walk around like males. We create a mess and we don't clean it up. The whole aspect of leaning on or depending on something else to sustain you as a man is totally opposite of what you are taught. As a man you're taught to be the provider and a protector, but in the kingdom you're taught to allow God to protect you and be your provider just by following his footsteps. So in your manly nature, on a daily basis, you try to find ways to do things on your own. You try to be a man in the way the world says be the man, not realizing that the stronger you are is when you're most humbled, when you're really dependent on God. It's like a baby. The baby is most dependent on a mother for nurturing. That is the way God wants us to be. We are always taught to have this hard, tough shell because we are men. You are not supposed to express your emotions, but it's not necessarily the truth. I think it is quite the opposite. You're more of a man when you can admit your wrongs, when you can admit your emotions, and express yourself because it shows sensitivity and you are walking in the image of our Father. He is sensitive. He's not hard, so it is almost like an oxymoron. The way I carry this out on a daily basis – I have some good days and I have some bad days – I don't get too high and I don't get too low. I try to put myself in a situation where I am always listening. I try to be sensitive of what the spirit is saying to me from the time I wake up in the morning to what I am wearing. Some may think that is crazy but that is the way I operate. He speaks and says, "No, don't wear that," or "Go to the bank and get money out." I don't know why but I will just do it. Then down the line, later in the day it is like, "Oh wow, this is what this was for." It basically teaches you how to be independent, but not quite at the same time, if that makes any sense.

Tell me why you couldn't imagine your life without God.

Wow. I would be so lost. I like to say that God is like my cheat sheet. In school we had a cheat sheet to pass a test. God is the ultimate cheat sheet. There are certain things that you didn't see coming but he warned you, and whether you take heed to the warning or not, that's on you, but you can't say you didn't know it was coming. The most critical thing you can have in a war is sight and vision. If you have both sight and vision, you can be very effective. Without God there is no sight and without vision there is no peace. Life with no peace is very horrible. Peace is that calmness when everything around you is going crazy and life sometimes gets very crazy. Without God there is no way you're going to last, period. You will be devoured. God is essential. He is like air; He is life. You can't even describe life without Him, it's just not going to happen. To answer your question, there is no life.

Men have a lot to live up to in the Bible as husbands according to Ephesians 5:21-33. Is it difficult to live up to these standards now as a husband or when you decide to marry? Why?

I don't think it is difficult nor do I think it is impossible, but I do think it is a process. The Bible says that husbands are to love their wives like Christ loved the church. Which means that it is a perfect love, which almost doesn't make sense because you have to love your wife even if she is wrong or when she irks your nerves. You still have to master your emotions and be able to love her with a sense of love that is overwhelming. As a husband, the strongest thing and the greatest characteristic is love, but in order to give that you have to know what it is. If you really know how God loves you, you can reciprocate that to others. That is why I don't think it is impossible to do, but I do feel that it is a very strenuous process because a lot of times we really don't understand love. We think about love in a way that says, what does it profit me? What am I getting from this? Love is selfless. You don't think about *you* when you love, you love hard. No one has to earn love from you, you just give it; it's a gift. It doesn't make any sense because now I have to lose sight of my feelings because I have to love you in spite of anything. That in itself is not easy. Being a husband like the Bible says is a job in itself. A lot of women say it's easy, but a lot of women are on a whole different scale. You have to understand every emotion there is on a daily basis. Sometimes the women themselves don't understand what that emotion is, but you have to be able to deal with that and still love them consistently. It's a lot of work. (He laughs.)

If you could describe your relationship with God, what would you say about it? How does it help you day to day?

I would describe it as night and day. He being night and I am day. It works and it blends together. God and I together are a great match, but there are times when I feel like, "Alright, OK, I got this!" Then God looks at you and he's like, "OK! Go ahead!" Then I will come back like, "Ugggh!" He is like, "Come here!" (Gestures to be pulled in for a hug). I am very hard on myself and I expect a lot, so God keeps me balanced. We are truly like night and day. We blend together perfectly, but God is just my best friend, my diary. I can talk to him about the craziest stuff and he just listens. I can say stuff that'll have someone like, "What!" But instead I talk to God because he is always there; he is consistent. Our relationship is unique in itself. There is not a day that goes by that I cannot talk to him. If I wake up in the morning and I don't spend time with him, my whole day is off. The way I treat it now, because I am a single man, I treat it like a relationship with a higher significance on it. You wake up, you say good morning, have a conversation, and have breakfast together. You may go to work, you go on lunch break and you might call him. You come home and you want to talk about your day. It is the same way with God. When I go to sleep at night, I basically talk to him and that is basically it.

Tell me, what is the most valuable lesson you have learned summed up in one sentence?

"I'd rather tolerate the pain of their absence than the consequence of their presence."

Basically meaning, there are a lot of things that come into our lives that we can choose to deal with or not deal with. Anything that is a distraction when it comes to things of God shouldn't be there. I had to learn that. The pain of not having someone there or not having certain things in life, I would rather deal with that than having the consequence of having them there and not having the direction of God, or walking in the favor of God, or in obedience to God, or walking in the peace of God because I am walking upright before God. That is the best way I can describe it.

****

There are so many powerful statements in this testimony, it really makes you think about your life as you are reading it. Once again, we come across someone who was a people pleaser and never really cared about himself. He was always putting people first. At some point in life we realize that we put too much energy into others and not enough into ourselves.

I too went through a phase of singleness for two years. During those two years, I allowed God to show me all the things that haunted me on a daily basis about who I was and where I wanted to be as an individual. My ex often said things to me that weren't always the nicest, but he was very frank and no one had ever talked to me that way – things that allowed me to evaluate my character and decide if I was truly ready to be someone's wife let alone co-worker because my attitude was so bad. In some aspect, people were "people-pleasing" me when I truly wanted honesty, yet I couldn't handle it. Once God started revealing things to me and showing me how to become mild mannered and gradually start listening to what people said rather than reacting immediately off trigger words, I became this person who everyone was super in awe of. I didn't see the process overnight, but I only recognized it because people saw it and kept apologizing for the way they reacted when asking for advice because I didn't react the way I used to. I had no clue that I had a sense of peace in the middle of a storm, and that is why Jesus sleeping in the middle of a storm is so profound to me. I indeed was a baby Jesus during one of the most prolific times of my life, yet it was one of the most emotional times as well. God is able.

The relationship I have built with God is irreplaceable. During that time of my life I did not want people to see me as weak or heartbroken because there was so much positive going on at the same time. When in reality, I wanted to cry myself to sleep all day, every day. God didn't let me. His still, small voice was so loud and He said: "Why are you crying when the greatest form of love comes from ME?" I never cried over my relationship again. When I felt weak, I talked to God. When I felt that the pressure was too much, I talked to God. When I saw my ex, God said to me: "Keep smiling, say hello, keep your head raised high, keep smiling because I have made you well." Lord did he! It was scary to live it because I didn't want to do that, but God encouraged me to do so. To this day, I have no idea how I made it through such a difficult breakup, but my relationship with God kept me going. I will forever and always be grateful for that. I know there may be many more trials to come, but my loyalty was made firm – concrete even – off that one situation.

Both men and women alike have a yearning to partner with someone who will bring them happiness and eventually, love. In order to give that type of love, we have to understand the love that God has for us first. Mark my words: There is no greater love, there really isn't. If you're not married it may come from your parents after God. If you are married, then it'll come from your spouse after God. There is no greater love, He trumps all.

4 Love suffers long and is kind; love does not envy; love does not parade itself, is not puffed up; 5 does not behave rudely, does not seek its own, is not provoked, thinks no evil; 6 does not rejoice in iniquity, but rejoices in the truth; 7 bears all things, believes all things, hopes all things, endures all things.

8 Love never fails. But whether there are prophecies, they will fail; whether there are tongues, they will cease; whether there is knowledge, it will vanish away. 9 For we know in part and we prophesy in part. 10 But when that which is perfect has come, then that which is in part will be done away.

11 When I was a child, I spoke as a child, I understood as a child, I thought as a child; but when I became a man, I put away childish things. 12 For now we see in a mirror, dimly, but then face to face. Now I know in part, but then I shall know just as I also am known.

13 And now abide faith, hope, love, these three; but the greatest of these is love.

1 Corinthians 13:4-13

Amen.

When I Thought I Was Alone –

That Was When God Was the Closest

Age: 35

Customer Service Representative

"Yea, though I walk through the valley of
the shadow of death,
I will fear no evil;
For You *are* with me;
Your rod and Your staff, they comfort me."

(Psalms 23:4)

Tell me what was your life like before Christ?

Before Christ, my life had an incomplete feeling to it. I questioned "my purpose" often, but the funny thing is that I always felt that there was a reason for my life, as I always believed there was a purpose for everyone in this world to play.

I didn't really understand the role Jesus had in my life and what exactly he had completed as my savior. So many of my choices in life were very different from what they are today. I tried to fill an empty feeling I used to feel by sexual experiences with females, surrounding myself in areas that weren't really the best of places, and getting caught up with things that didn't serve a positive role in my life.

I don't remember an exact date, but roughly around 1995-96, I was with one of my cousins hanging out one evening. We were headed to an area where we would hang out often. It was a low-income housing community, but to us it was where we'd go to fill the boredom that chased us. Well that particular evening, on the way there, I felt an uneasy feeling. Something kept urging me not to go there and to go somewhere else instead. So I threw the idea of going to my house, throwing in some movies, and keeping it simple that evening. Back then we didn't own cars and always had to consider catching a cab if we were too tired to walk or couldn't get a ride. So my cousin agreed on keeping it a simple evening.

A few hours later, I got paged on a beeper I had then, and when I returned the call I was told that there had been a shooting. Unfortunately I knew people from both sides of the disagreement, but never knew the complete story of what happened. There were so many different versions and views from people that all you could do was assume what had occurred with your own mental picture. But one thing that didn't have to be assumed was the outcome. There was a person killed and two others shot. Immediately when I heard the news it brought me back to that feeling that I felt so strong on my way up there. Until this day, the fellas that were involved in that situation are behind bars. I know it was God changing the path that I was on that evening to protect me from what was ahead of it. Until this day, I think to myself how different my life would've been if I didn't listen to that feeling? I could've been behind bars or even worse, underground!

What does your salvation mean to you?

Salvation to me is something that I have learned to appreciate and be grateful for. It's life over death. Choosing to accept that we are forgiven for all of our sins through Jesus being that perfect sacrifice. That if we accept Jesus as our Lord and Savior, that God looks upon us through the accomplishments of what Jesus completed instead of our failures and sins that we have committed.

We don't have to be perfect because, in God's view, we are through what Jesus completed on the cross on our behalf. With that being said, I know it doesn't mean to go out and sin, it simply brings that peace to me knowing that with his word and working on my faith God will make sure, at the end of it all, things will be OK. I thank you God for loving me throughout it all.

If you could save someone by telling them one thing God has done for you in your life, what would it be?

Throughout many years of my life, I always felt a feeling of emptiness. I can't really even describe the feeling completely. But a type of lonely feeling that hindered me, even in a crowded room. I had reached a point in my life where I knew I needed to make changes. Some areas needed big changes, as others just a tad bit. But change was definitely needed.

At the time, I dated someone that went to church and had made a decision in her life some time before to make her changes. I saw how she was mainly in a good mood and saw things in a positive light, which was something that I wanted to share and have in my life as well. When I questioned her about being in a good mood and seeming as if she didn't have worries, she replied by saying that going to church refueled her faith in knowing that God would make all things right. The pastor's message would make her feel good. I really didn't understand completely, but little did I know that a few months later I'd start going to the same church and I'm still going to Faith Fellowship Ministries in Sayreville, NJ.

Basically with that being said, it's up to only *you* to make the choice of change if you feel you want better in your life. I'm not saying it's always easy, but with different choices will come different outcomes along your path. Start with small things for example, reading a little more, or what exactly are you reading? Is it something that will benefit your life in a positive manner? Small changes will lead to big outcomes without one even realizing it.

Describe some of the daily pressures you have to face as a godly man and how do you overcome them?

Something I face on a daily is controlling my temper and just not reacting at first impulse. Throughout my younger years, a lot of things instilled images and certain directions about how things should be in life that I view completely different now. Music, television, games, and various other things influenced my choices and decisions that I would make growing up. Of course my parents and family also held their share of weight in my decisions. But overall, music really did influence me on ways I viewed relationships, the purpose of money, and it induced a prideful demeanor instead of a humble one. Not that I'm trying to point blame for my actions and choices; but it sure had its influence and impact on my decisions.

Nowadays I practice being humble and I really try to put myself in the place of other people to see why they're saying or acting as they are instead of just allowing me to lose control of my peace. I have come to understand that the smallest altercation can become the biggest problem of many. With keeping my mind on God and his direction, it allows me to ignore many things and words that once allowed me to get out of character.

One of the things that has allowed me to become a better person and overcome pressures of my everyday life is trying to be mindful of the messages behind the music I listen to. I have started listening to a Christian rapper named Bizzle and can relate to the messages and views behind most of his songs. When I take a shower, I bring my cell phone and YouTube Bishop Dale Bronner and T.D. Jakes amongst others for a positive message. Their messages are inspiring and help me keep a creative mind to improve my life. I try to make time to read more than before, and try to be mindful on what I'm reading also. I believe everything in life has to have balance.

Tell me why you couldn't imagine your life without God.

It's funny, my life without God would be chaos filled with unhappiness, loneliness, sadness, anger, and I could go on. I once heard a message in a song by Bizzle saying something to the nature of: Study the truth and you'll see the lies, if you study the lies they'll just come up with new lies to mislead you. God's word is the truth, and the Bible will lead you to the path that you should be on.

God has brought peace from within to me. He has filled that emptiness that I once felt. He is slowly showing me direction in life. He has definitely helped me get out of some binds that I couldn't see the end to, financially and spiritually. I have learned about his grace, love, and that things do happen in his timing and not mine. So in other words, I'm learning how to work on my patience. I'm surrounding myself in new environments and also meeting others who show more meaning in my life and my purpose. I'm still a growing child in Christ. But every day is a new experience for improvement, and of course, knowing I'm a blessed child of Christ.

Men have a lot to live up to in the Bible as husbands according to Ephesians 5:21-33. Is it difficult to live up to these standards now as a husband or when you decide to marry? Why?

I'm not married but I do believe when the time comes, even through all of the challenges I'll be facing, God will lead me down the right path. It will be a path of growth and lessons to be learned to become even a better husband and overall, man of God.

If you could describe your relationship with God, what would you say about it? How does it help you day to day?

My relationship with God is definitely a growing one daily. I know I'm far from perfect and continue to make mistakes. But now, instead of beating myself up about them, I try to focus more on learning from them. I know that God speaks to me by other people, feelings, thoughts, and simply at times by just standing still, and yes at times, literally standing still. A moment to thank God for everything I do have that I don't show enough appreciation for. For example, having a family that shows support even during moments of vulnerability. I am blessed with health and a body to accomplish what I need to do daily. I am mindful that in certain parts of the world they don't have the option to just turn a faucet and have water come out of it. Sometimes miles have to be walked to be able to have the pleasures of a simple glass of water. So yes, I try to make it my business to thank God every day, if not several times a day, for what I've been blessed with. Sometimes we lose sight of what really is important in life! So thank you Heavenly Father for all that I have been blessed with, including loved ones, friends, and even those that have provided me a lesson to allow me to become a better person to help others that cross my path. Thank You!

Tell me, what is the most valuable lesson you have learned summed up in one sentence?

No matter what anyone is going through, God's love can overcome anything if you allow his love into your heart. Have faith.

****

The smallest altercation can lead to a bigger problem. That jumped out of the page for me. How many times have you taken something someone has said to you to heart? It pierced a little more than it should have. Usually it wouldn't have, but it did. Sometimes that can be a breaking point or even the end of a friendship.

Many times we go through life expecting things to go our way all of the time. Things almost never go as planned. There are also some bumps in the road that hinder us from getting across the finish line, but eventually we get there, someway, somehow. It may take days, weeks, months, or years in fact, but it happens. These bumps in the road allow us to go through a process we would have never seen coming. The process that makes us go off course toward the dirt road instead of the shiny new paved one. There is the distraction that causes a reaction to the things that appear shiny. Shiny is designed to steer us away from God's goal – our goal and our path toward destiny. It is in fact difficult to not want to go toward that bright, shiny object because it seems so easy to obtain. The thing about God is, nothing is ever too easy. One has to work for it. The work produces a harvest bigger than we could have achieved on our own. I often say that God is a god of the impossible, but what I really mean is he can take someone who is completely afraid of public speaking and give him or her a platform to sow into people's lives on a daily basis, which at times involves public speaking. That is something impossible to someone who has a fear of public speaking.

Anything can be achieved with God. We must remain steadfast, awake, and alert because He is always speaking to us; we have to hear him just like this young man did. He avoided death or possible life in prison for being at the wrong place at the wrong time. The Holy Spirit was able to guide him before he even dedicated his life solely to God. That alone goes to show you that God is love and He loves his children. He is always looking out for us. We may not make the right decisions, but that doesn't mean he didn't attempt to direct our paths.

We each have a special gift in us that God has hand-crafted us with. It is vital to tap into that gift or gifts in order to fulfill our destiny. Many often ask what their life's purpose is. I've even had people ask me what I think their life's purpose is because I seemed to have found mine. My only advice is this: spend time with the Lord, ask him to first reveal that purpose to you, and then ask him to prepare you for it so that you are ready and you are prepared for the rewards and challenges that come along with it. Prayer works.

Dear Man of God,

After reading your testimony, all I can say is wow, look at what the Lord has done for you!

Did you know that the greatest amount of faith anyone could have wouldn't be for material things or for things that give you temporary pleasure, but it would be in choosing to believe that Jesus Christ is Lord over your life? The moment you believe it, your eyes open, your ears sharpen, your heart changes, and your actions start to transform you into a new being walking in a new direction, which is the "right direction."

You went from being an ordinary man to becoming an extraordinary man for the one sole reason that you decided to accept Christ as part of your identity. Today, many people suffer from having an identity crisis, but yours is wrapped up in where Christ is. This is something worth being excited about because your swag doesn't reflect a jaded image that doesn't know where it's going, neither here nor there, it's one that is now polished with a newfound confidence that you now know who you *really* are, and that you are no longer

75

confused about where you stand as a man in this crazy, directionless world. You are now purpose-driven, bold, and courageous to step out to make a difference and be the compass that leads others in the right direction. It seems like a daunting and overwhelming responsibility for you, but God has already given you all the necessary ingredients to fulfill your purpose in life, which is to be a leader and one who leads others to where God wants them to be. I'm not promising you it'll be easy, but I will say that with God on your side, all things that you want to do are possible if you just don't give up.

No, it doesn't mean you are perfect, or that you will always have it put together. However, you remain an extraordinary man because you are now a man of God simply because you decided to say goodbye to the past you, the one who was in pain and was dissatisfied with what life had to offer, which seemed like nothing, and have welcomed yourself to the renewed you, who has embraced a powerful future with God on your side.

You are no longer traveling life feeling lost, confused, and all alone, even though loneliness is a common feeling anyone can feel when traveling a journey of a thousand miles. God has always been with you from the very beginning and will continue to be in your life's journey until the very end. He will be there for you through the thick and thin, and He will not abandon you nor leave you hanging like so many others may have in your life who disappointed you or let you down. Just remember this:

> **Deuteronomy 31:8** - The Lord himself goes before you and will be with you; he will never leave you nor forsake you. Do not be afraid; do not be discouraged."

Yes, you will encounter various battles in your walk, that's something that can't be avoided, but you must go through them in order to come out stronger. You must learn from mistakes made and grow from them. That's the only way to experience maturity. The world has so many different versions and definitions to define what a *real* man is, but a man who fears God is worthy of praise and should get noticed. Nothing can keep you from the love of God, just as the Bible says:

> **Romans 8:38-39 -** [38] For I am persuaded that neither death nor life, nor angels nor principalities nor powers, nor things present nor things to come, [39] nor height nor depth, nor any other created thing, shall be able to separate us from the love of God which is in Christ Jesus our Lord.

As a God-fearing Christian man, you will stand out from the rest. You are unique, you are outstanding, you will outshine others, you will be the answer to many important questions, and you will be sought out and sought after because you are now the light that shines in the darkness that other people are trapped in just because you now have Christ in you, the hope of glory.

A life without Christ is like running on empty. Unfortunately, not many people realize that is their status quo. With Christ, you can refuel, rejuvenate, and rejoice because he is now your strength during the times you feel weakest. He is the lifter of your head when you are feeling down, and He is the one who shows you which way you ought to go for the times when you feel lost and confused.

The greatest thing for you to do right now is to keep on pressing forward while staying focused on what's ahead of you and never look back (at your past). Looking back serves you no purpose than to be reminded of what you once were, whereas facing what's right in front of you serves to keep you pursuing what you want to hold onto right now. You are now holding onto the hope you have, which is in Christ Jesus. I encourage you to share that hope with others, because if you don't, who else will? Just as the word says:

1 Peter 3:14-16 -[14] But even if you should suffer

for what is right, you are blessed. "Do not fear their threats; do not be frightened." [15] But in your hearts revere Christ as Lord. Always be prepared to give an answer to everyone who asks you to give the reason for the hope that you have. But do this with gentleness and respect, [16] keeping a clear conscience, so that those who speak maliciously against your good behavior in Christ may be ashamed of their slander.

Your life is a testimony of God's saving grace. You could have been dead and gone, but Christ kept you. This is the story people want to hear about, or should I say *need* to hear about, the story in which many people take their own lives for granted because they simply think they can just walk around and do life anyway and anyhow, and live long enough to enjoy it. You lost someone you knew who thought this way, but you now have the ability to take this knowledge of the truth to impact others and let them know there is something more to life than just this, that there is something much bigger out there than just us, and *that* something happens to be Jesus Christ.

Standing up for what you believe in is the first step of sharing the hope that you have in Jesus to others. It doesn't matter if people ridicule you. Your faith is what makes you stronger and steadfast in your walk. Many talk the walk, but don't walk the talk. You are different, so I encourage you to continue to thank God for each day that you have. You have just ended a journey in which you have walked many miles feeling alone to now having a life-long partner, Jesus Christ, walk with you as you move from strength to strength and from faith to faith.

> **Psalm 31:24 -** Be of good courage, And He shall strengthen your heart, All you who hope in the Lord.

Keep your head up and God bless you on your journey my friend,

Blessings from your sister in Christ.

****

This letter was written by a young lady whose testimony was in *The Past is in the Past so Let it Pass: For Women* for the young man on the previous page. See her testimony "Out From Darkness" on page 57 of *The Past is in the Past so Let it Pass: For Women.*

Mr. Transformed

Age: 34

Retail/Property Management

"And do not be conformed to this world, but be transformed by the renewing of your mind, that you may prove what *is* that good and acceptable and perfect will of God"

(Romans 12:2)

Tell me what was your life like before Christ?

There was a time in my life when I thought I could do everything on my own. I later found out that it was called a male complex. I soon thereafter found out that we as Christians were created to worship God and that everything we could possibly need revolved around a relationship with him. The biggest reality was when I realized that if my relationship with him was suffering, my relationships everywhere else were challenged with suffering also. I quickly began to realize that God is a jealous God. If I was created to worship and have a relationship with Christ, and I am choosing everything else on my own to satisfy and fulfill my life, then nothing I could have possibly done had the chance or opportunity for longevity. I quickly got to the point where I began to question why things seemed to work, and then all of a sudden they didn't. I would get jobs and then get fired. I would meet what I thought at the time was the nicest of women, and then get hurt so blindly. Everything seemed to go right for a moment, and then go horribly wrong. I began to question my "know it all" self, saying things like, "What did you do wrong? Did you love her? Check. Did you do the best job you could have possibly done? Check. Did you cherish her and show her that you are a real gentleman? Check and check. What the heck went wrong then?" I realized my relationship with Christ was starving, therefore, my natural desires starved.

What does your salvation mean to you?

It's cliché, but everything. I would be consumed by this world if Jesus did not die on the cross; he died so that I may live. And live a life free from condemnation. Now as a teen, I played or attempted to play baseball for my varsity high school team, but for some reason or another when the ball would reach me from a pass or line drive, I dropped the ball at the worst of times, losing games, being the laughingstock, ridiculed, and shunned because of this. I had a long talk with my mother at the end of my promising career in high school baseball: "Baby-boy," she would call me, "... if Jesus didn't make it to the Promised Land before being beat and bruised spit on and stabbed by the same ones who claimed to love him, what makes you think you're getting off scot-free?" That conversation changed my whole perspective on why he died for me. He died so that I can live and not be cast out and shunned. It lets me know that he can magnanimously take someone who dropped the ball, like the boy with glasses, or use the murderer or drug dealer/user, and turn what they view as trash and a crap quality of life, and use it for his glory...but God.

If you could save someone by telling them one thing God has done for you in your life, what would it be?

If I could help save a life, marriage, or struggling relationship, I would tell them about my testimony about how God saved me, saved my mind so that I can live to tell and show the power that God has given each and every one of us. The best part of being in a relationship with God is realizing that in order to see yourself blessed and highly favored, you must position yourself to be blessed, position yourself to receive his wisdom, and position yourself to receive his favor. Otherwise, you're going to die thinking you know everything. And that's not even half of what God has in store. Ears have not heard nor eyes seen...

Describe some of the daily pressures you have to face as a godly man and how do you overcome them?

I am currently seeing a counselor who is so passionate about operating in a functional relationship with Christ and it's so profound because there are exercises that direct you right to the Bible for direction in situations like:

"Should I get with this girl or should I stay focused; or should I speak this way to women, or steal, or mishandle certain things that come my way." It's not just about saying I want to walk right, I want to do right, yeah! Or, today I got saved in front of the church and got my ticket to heaven, yeah. No, you must practice daily what you believe to be true by praying, fasting, trusting, and having faith. But most of all you must actively have a plan on how to apply his word to your life.

Tell me why you couldn't imagine your life without God.

I would be under the biggest rock somewhere if I didn't know who my God is. The weight and the pressure of this world would have crushed my mind, then my body, then my soul. I thank God for loving me so. I have had a lonely life without him; even though he was with me, I didn't know him. I would be lost (without him), in a box with toys no one ever wanted to play with again. I honestly don't want to ever imagine life without him again.

Men have a lot to live up to in the Bible as husbands according to Ephesians 5:21-33.

Is it difficult to live up to these standards now as a husband or when you decide to marry? Why?

As a divorced husband, at first I found it difficult to live up to the standards of great men of the Bible. But that was before I understood that, as a man, you can never completely understand your wife. That's why you must study her daily. I have come to terms with making every attempt to study her and show myself approved for her. When you do not understand the job at hand, then you are bound to fail. Women need consistency from men, and in order to provide that you must study, learn, and understand her, but when you think you understand her, start over and learn her again. Women are so beautifully complex. A woman can be compared to a DNA gene – these genes were custom-made by none other than God himself. If he can create something as fine as DNA, why would he create her? And she is fine and worth loving and caring and being patient for and understanding and strength, so before you accept this mission you must understand the job responsibilities and prerequisites.

If you could describe your relationship with God, what would you say about it? How does it help you day to day?

I am striving for the father-son relationship with God. As a man, I struggled with putting my pride down to ask God for help. At times I was mad and selfish and angry with God. But I began to realize that it's not just a worship experience he desires from us. He wants an intimate relationship with you. And as I get closer to him, I realize that at times I must come to him child-like, free, and empty of myself. And as a grown man, this is still something I am working on to this day. But something I challenge other men to do is if you don't know how to empty yourself, ask God. He will definitely show you.

Tell me, what is the most valuable lesson you have learned summed up in one sentence?

"I can do all things through Christ who strengthens me."

We are created by God, but the enemy wants to convince us that we suck and you're a horrible person because you did x, y, z. But the biggest trick of the enemy is trying to convince you that you can't. We weren't created to "can't." You've got the power; you've got the touch, from *Transformers* the movie.

****

There isn't one person in this book who has not started from the bottom and worked his way up toward God; even the ones who have been in church their entire lives, much like myself. It is like riding a bike with training wheels, but the training wheels never come off until we are in a good standing relationship with God. Eventually the training wheels come off and, at times, our bikes need to be readjusted, then the training wheels come back on. Different roads require different wheels, much like the snow requires snow tires. I do not care if you have been serving God for 55 years, you will still need his help. For those who are not believers, you are probably familiar with the *Footprints* prayer where you notice two sets of footprints then you only notice one. The author asks the question to the Lord: "You said that if I followed you, you would walk with me," then the Lord responds, "During the low years of your life I carried you!" The Lord will always be there, even when it doesn't feel like he is there. What a great God! One of my favorite scriptures is Psalm 138:8, "The Lord will perfect that which concerns me; Your mercy, O Lord, endures forever; Do not forsake the works of Your hands" (NKJV). However, I love the Message Bible's version of this verse because it just goes to show you the promise that God has made with us through the sacrifice of his son, Christ Jesus. It reads:

> *When I walk into the thick of trouble,*
> *keep me alive in the angry turmoil.*
> *With one hand*
> *strike my foes,*
> *With your other hand*
> *save me.*
> *Finish what you started in me, GOD.*
> *Your love is eternal—don't quit on me now.*

If God can be there for both you and me at the same time, why can't we give him all the honor and all the glory he deserves?

Men Made By Mercy

Age: 42

Minister, Counselor, Occupational Therapist, Fitness Instructor,

Event Coordinator, Entertainer, and Dancer/Choreographer

"Oh, give thanks to the LORD, for *He is* good!
For His mercy *endures* forever."

(Psalms 107:1)

Tell me what was your life like before Christ?

Maniacal crazy. I was all about dance battles in the club, deep house music, Barbara Tucker, big shoes, dreads, funky polka dots, suspenders, entertainment, step shows with my fraternity, Mr. Popularity, very loud, rambunctious, didn't do drugs back then – really enough – I drank a little bit, but that wasn't my source of getting high. My high was the dance. I spent my days in the projects in

Queens. It was all about the dance, all about the step shows, all about the practices and rehearsals – it was all about me. Relationships – I had them, but I didn't know how to nurture them because I was magnifying dance. Dance was my relationship.

I always had a love, an affinity, attachment, and deep relationship with God. I always had a love for God. In fact, I grew up in a household where there were three women and one stepfather. Out of everyone in that household I was the one who they made go to church. I was the only one, so on a Sunday morning everyone is in bed, my mother is ironing my clothes and making me go to church. I was the youngest out of everyone in the house: my sisters are in bed, my stepfather is in bed, and my mother was ironing my clothes and making breakfast for me. I was the one that had to go to church. I didn't understand it, but God did. So growing up in the absence of Christ, I was thugged out – a little thugged-out dancer – not too smart, not too witty. In a corporate environment I was very passive aggressive, very quiet. I had a lot to say, which I was afraid to say what I needed to say because I wasn't sure if it was going to be received or not. I was very timid, so much so that when the summit came for me to accept Christ as my Lord and Savior, all my fears and anxieties came to the forefront so much that it became crippling.

I was in bondage to fear for three and a half years. At the inception of me giving my life to Christ, that was in truth what brought me to Christ, the attack of this spirit of fear. Waking up shaking every single second of the day, I didn't understand it. I was breaking out in hives, having panic attacks, having anxiety attacks. It was so excessive my co-workers began to see it and noticed my hands were always shaking. At that point it became uncontrollable. That was a hellish component. The only thing that stopped me from committing suicide at the brink of my salvation was that I knew I would not see God. I had such a great love for him, I knew enough to know that if I had taken my own life, I would forfeit my accessibility to see God, and so I didn't. I fought through the fears. Every single second of the day I had to quote 2 Timothy 1:7, "For God has not given us a spirit of fear, but of power and of love and of a sound mind." I have the mind of Christ; cast all your cares upon Him because He cares for you. Every single second of the day I had to meditate on scripture in spite of what I felt. I could quote scripture and yet I'm shaking, breaking out, heart beating like 500 miles per hour, waking up in the morning and the assault would begin immediately. As soon as I would open my eyes it would happen immediately.

My life before Christ was filled with a lot of spiritual warfare from ages nine through 12. I mean I would see demons every other day as a child. (They would come) into my room, banging on my bed, pinning me down – can't move, can't talk. It was crazy. My parents weren't spiritually inclined to be able to handle what I was going through so I was told, "Go to bed, stop eating that sugar, stop eating that, stop eating this, leave me alone boy!" I went through a lot – alone.

Now one night in particular I woke up to being dragged down a hall in such a darkness I have never ever seen before in my life. It was a darkness that superseded anything in the natural realm. It was dark! I am being dragged down the hall by my feet, and before I knew it I was back in my body, and I jumped up and began to weep. I did not know what the hell was going on. I kept saying, "Oh my God, what happened; what is happening to me?" The following night, a whole entourage showed up in my room, demons, and there was one in particular standing by my armoire. He stood there leaning; he was different from all the other ones, I believe that was Satan himself wanting to know what in the world happened ("What happened? We had this individual who was on his way to hell. What happened?"). While all this was transpiring, I remember my Bible being on my nightstand. Now my body is pinned down, but I didn't know back then that your spirit man never sleeps, so now I am marveling because I am seeing two hands. My natural hand is stationary and my spirit hand is trying to move. I am still pinned down, and from the base of my forehead a white candle began to materialize. Once it got all the way to the wick, they all fled out of my room. I jumped up and I began to weep. I had no idea what was transpiring in my life. I knew I wasn't going crazy. I knew the spiritual warfare, but I didn't know how to fight. Then God began to lead me to scriptures. He said, "The spirit of man is a candle of the Lord" (Proverbs 20:27). When he told me that, I knew I was OK. From that point on, I was reading scripture and warring with them at night. It was straight warfare, warfare, warfare, warfare, all day long, warfare. They were relentless; they began to attack me in the day time. I went to lie down one day to take a nap, and it was a different caliber of demon who had entered into my room with an entourage. I had saw them looking decrepit, oh my gosh, anything that you see in the movies isn't far from the truth as far as what they look like and how they conduct themselves. We are nothing but conduits to the spiritual realm governed by our heart's conditions. If our hearts aren't tied to God, they are tied to the other one, so we become a manifestation of what is really out there, visually speaking. But at any rate, they were a different caliber, they were wicked, very wicked. My ceiling opened up and now I noticed three guys coming in on winged horses in a formation that you can tell they were strategically measured from the point of the two, to the two in the back and across, it was a perfect measure. They were coming, wings flapping simultaneously, unbothered in their faces. When this happened the demons fled from every which way. The ceiling closed up, I jumped up, and now I was weeping again.

Anything that happened to me spiritually was indicative of fatherlessness, I believe. My real father did not find out he was my real father until the age I was bar mitzvah'd. My mother finally told me that my stepfather was not my real father and called my real father on the phone at the age of 13 to introduce me to him. So for 13 years I believed my stepfather was my real father. I ended up taking on his last name in the name of fear because she was afraid of exposing the truth to me, so I took on my stepfather's last name. All because of her fear – my birth father may have known but I personally did not know. My stepdad treated me horribly all my years growing up.

In college, I had pledged (a fraternity) and that is when the homosexuality came in. So here I am pledging and the one who pledged me stepped to me (came on to me). Vulnerable and not clear of who I was, I yielded and submitted – I was done. I went into a state of depression like you wouldn't believe. In my room, door shut, I did not come out, but my mother – I love my mother a lot – but she wasn't equipped. She wasn't a conversationalist; she wasn't a communicator. I love her but it was like very tyrannical to some degree. It was, "do this, do that, do this, do that, or I will beat you; do this, do that, I love you," but she was the mother and the father of the house so she ruled with an iron fist. She didn't know how to communicate with me nor did I know how to communicate how I felt. I had to deal with that. Now that I had dealt with that, I became desensitized to it all. Then I finally said, "You know what, I am going full fledge with this homosexual thing." So I went for a while, but I was still asking God, "Lord God, what am I doing?" Then the fear kicked in. That is when I began to pursue God.

A lot has transpired in my life. I have every right to be nasty, bitter, and angry. I am not that way because of God. At some point I had to address my mother on a lot of stuff. I was molested at the age of 5 by my mother. I carried that weight on me for 35 years – by myself. Every five years or so I would get a best girl/homegirl. This one young lady specifically was my student as I was her dance instructor. She became much older and we grew exceptionally close. People thought we were in a relationship together but we weren't. We were really best friends. As she and I grew in the Lord, she said to me, "You have to confront your mother!" In 2007, I confronted my mother, she denied it, and my family ostracized me. They made me feel like the victim, and I remember feeling alone. I felt so alone. This was after I was married. I just wanted my mother to say she was sorry; I never wanted to hear anything else, just sorry. I knew she knew it was wrong, but that was all I wanted. Don't' make me the scapegoat of your ineptitude, just say sorry. You did this, now I have to become penalized because of what you did. How can you say you love me when love is selfless, yet you chose to exalt yourself over the one you inflicted this caliber of injustice upon? Girl, you could've been locked up! I forgave her. I had to. It took my time with FITS (Faith International Training School) in 2009.

In 1995, I got married to a super intellectual, the epitome of intelligence, scholastically inclined, beautiful, drop-dead gorgeous, studied abroad woman. She was very corporate: Lehman Brothers, Goldman Sachs, Rockefeller Foundation, she was up there. For me, I am not-for-profit. There was a bitterness that this woman had with her family. One thing I learned in life is how you leave one environment not healed, you will enter into the next environment extremely bitter and blaming the next person for everything. We used to fight like you wouldn't believe. I was dumb. After being saved two years before that, going through all of the spiritual and fear attacks, and finally reading my Bible, I took the word literally. I did not understand all the feuds and bickering and why she was mad. I knew it wasn't scriptural. It was a rude awakening when I realized that people aren't fully committed to this word. I was hurting. That relationship with her almost destroyed me. I was a yes man. Far from what I am now, you had it as soon as you asked it. You were my wife, it was always yes, yes, yes, yes. There was no argument here. I don't like arguing; I don't like being angry. I had no argument. People would ask and I would ask myself, "Why aren't you angry?" I didn't know what it was to be angry.

After seeing what God has done for me, I look back and all I can say is, wow, he is an awesome God. He is faithful, amazing, and I am grateful.

Men have a lot to live up to in the Bible as husbands according to Ephesians 5:21-33. Is it difficult to live up to these standards now as a husband or when you decide to marry? Why?

It was never hard. I love God, and my joy is other people's success. That has always brought joy to my heart, but in my past relationship, she was so caught up in her emotions and anger that if I didn't react, my actions were contrite, as if I wasn't living up to my real feelings, or I was accused of being fake or phony. Meanwhile, I had to force myself from feelings and had to live according to the word. She, on the other hand, continued to call me phony and a counterfeit in my thought process because I wasn't reacting with her. My joy is to always love and show respect. But one thing about a man and a woman, a woman needs to be valued; she wants to know that you understand her feelings and understand her emotions, which then adds value. A man needs respect, period.

At the inception of this marital union, I was emasculated. For example, we had just gotten home and her witchcraft behavior went into full effect. I was like her mother again and she was herself. It was something as miniscule as buying a jar of mayonnaise. We had just gotten back home from our honeymoon, and I had asked her to get the big jar of mayonnaise at the store because, in my mind, mayonnaise lasts forever. She yells, "Get the small one!" I said, "No, just get the big one. It's mayonnaise, it doesn't expire." She went from zero to 60, screaming out every derogatory term to attack me with. Now I am in the store galvanized because, first off, her friend is there. Second, we are in a public place and people are starting to stare. It was too much. I know everything starts in the spiritual realm then articulates itself into the natural realm. She was just an open vessel to my demise. She rattled off how I was dumb, stupid, immature, and I just sat there as passive as I was. I suffered from low self-esteem. I had just overcome all of the phobias. I was wounded and I just took it. I was destroyed.

Nowadays, I love everybody, but I am wise and I am so John Legend with it, "This time we will take it slow," because I want to see all the red flags and I want to take my time. If I don't keep my standards, I will be no good to anybody. In that past relationship I had rescinded all of my standards and became a doormat to this woman who was super intelligent, never at a loss for words. She was capable of verbally assassinating people; she was brutal. With her educational background, how could you not be? That evening we went home, and once we got in the bed I finally asked her: "Do you ever think about me and what you say before you say it?" She turned around and looked at me and said, "No!" She turned right back around and went to sleep. Mind you, this is the same exact night we came back from our honeymoon.

Feeling in a low place, I got up and went right to Manhattan. I didn't go to a club, I just started walking around the streets and started talking to God asking, "Lord God, what is this? Why? What is this? I just want to serve you!" We were engaged for two years, and during those two years I suffered from low self-esteem, not able to make proper decisions. I was so caught up in my own world and feelings that I was not able to properly assess what the relationship was and say, "You know what self, this is not it! I can't afford for someone to speak to me in this manner." We were able to answer everything correctly in our wedding counselor book; we were both smart. We knew the principles of God's word, so we were considered perfect for marriage. Meanwhile, our hearts were not aligned and we were destined for destruction. She was an angry woman. Anger is an emotion that is secondary to some kind of hurt. She was hurt growing up.

Once I returned home that night, it was about 4 a.m. and she jumped up asking where was I? The whole time my heart was all about love and respect because it was a marriage. This was my wife. She threw a file cabinet on me because she said it was unacceptable that I was gone for all that time. She said she didn't care what I was going through. We still had gifts from the wedding wrapped up, but one gift in particular was a large frame of the gifts of the spirit. She threw the entire picture at me. I should've known then. She screamed, "I hate you!!! I hate you!! I want a divorce!" I remember asking her over and over again, "What is going on? What is wrong with you? I love you, what is wrong with you?" But she just kept screaming the same things at me and hitting on me. Now I don't hit women at all, I was trying to get a hold of her and then she ran for my wardrobe. She started throwing stuff out the window and I faded to black. The road crew behind the scenes, you know the crew that really makes the scenes happen, I said, oh we are really about to make this scene happen. I'm about to go behind the scenes and make this scene happen on you. My clothes were on the street. I just bought that; I didn't even wear that yet. I lost it. I remember telling her, "Oh you want a divorce, you got it!" She didn't like that very much. She started going nuts. I refused to deal with it anymore; I was outta there and called the cops on her. The rest is history. After five years, that was it. God told me at the inception, you don't be no fool. At the inception of every action the story is told. I constantly watch people's gestures and actions to assess the story and then I decide whether or not I want to be a part of the story. With her, I was caught up in a horrific story. My last straw was when she told me that she wanted me to die and told me all of the ways that she wished I would die. I wanted to respect her but I ended up losing all respect for her. I lost the zeal of wanting to please her. I did not even know how to function myself any longer. I just overcame fear and now I had this going on in my life. It was too much. I was trying to manage ministry and the various ministries that I belonged to. I would minister to different people and then people would come up to me and thank me for giving them a word and she would be behind me saying, "Can you tell your cronies to leave! Can you tell your groupies to leave? Oh hi, I'm the wife." Hands down, I always wanted to love her like Christ loved the church, absolutely, but I didn't know what to do with that. At some point in time, everything that I did was wrong.

I haven't been in a relationship for the past 13 years.

I definitely said these women are crazy. I became a nasty, bitter, angry individual. I was able to get my bearings and just got up one day and moved from Brooklyn, NY, to Newark, NJ. My family did not know where I was. I ostracized myself from everybody. I was living crazy. I was mad. I was making crazy money, I got this loft in Newark and I said I was going to hook the place up, I was going to do me, and I am going full-fledged homo because I was done. I was so upset. I said I gave my heart to this chick and this is how she repaid me. I was done. Then one day my family found me. My sister found me. I was in my living room, no furniture in my apartment, watching *In Living Color* with a sweater on in the middle of summer. I was literally out of my mind, crazy. I heard banging on my door. It was my entire family, everyone crying. They thought I was dead. They didn't know what they were walking into. They thought I killed myself because I was missing in action for so long. Through all the craziness, God never stopped speaking to me, but before the pullback, he said to me: "Listen, I love you, but compromise is the root of demise." Once he said that, that grace that he had, he gradually started to pull back. The next day I had an eviction notice on my door. It got real crazy real fast. The guy I was dating was a thug. He had warrants out for his arrest. They had an entire swat team show up at my house looking for him. Meanwhile, he hadn't been there in three years. That was when the building manager was like, "Look you gotta go!" I was at an all-time low, low, low. My friend Chris was like, "Look you got to come back to Christ." That was when I really began my journey back, in 2007.

My next relationship, I can see it. I haven't been in a relationship for the past 10 years. But God is making it happen. It is going to be different though. This woman is going to be my best friend; she is going know everything about me. No surprises from soup to nuts. We can't be in the type of relationship that says, "I need to get out of the house to get away from you for a while." That is not love. I don't want to be away from the one that I love. This chick, whoever she is, will have to be my best friend. I have no problem respecting her and loving her. You need something? I got it, no problem. Whatever you sow selflessly, there is always multiplication to follow.

What does your salvation mean to you?

It means everything. It is my life. My life is salvation. Everything. He is my joy. He is my daddy. He is my peace, my wisdom. He is tribulation. Faith does not come from me, it comes from Him. He sits me down, gets in my face, and tells me not to write everything down, and I respond, "OK! It's so good though." I love him so much. I love his mercy. If I mess up, I hear him say, "My mercy is the endurance of my patience." What! Who says that? That's sick right there. "I endure you because I am patient. I am patient because I am merciful. My mercy is the endurance of my patience. I wait patiently because it's the process of your perfection. Why? Because I love you. I don't find fault, I continue to work with you." Jesus! Selah.

The reason why I am so merciful with the young adults is because there is nothing they can't call me about that I haven't done. I probably invented it (he laughs). But it is true. I want them to trust me and know that I am here for them. I am like their uncle. They gag when I tell them my age. I move better than half of them. I look great for my age. I praise God for allowing me to infiltrate the youth. They treat me as their peer. The wisdom that God drops they are accessible to it. It comes not with experience and persecution and a myriad of difficulty. I have been fortified by just loving Him through times of unusual difficulty, yet edifying Him.

Salvation is my life. It is my destiny and it is my dream come true.

Describe some of the daily pressures you have to face as a godly man and how do you overcome them?

Not giving in to emotion. Not giving devotion to my emotions. Having to always be in that place of meditation and the word. Keeping myself steadfast in a place of meditation and the word, allowing the word to supersede my feelings. If I can control how you feel, I can control your will. I have to magnify the word especially when it comes to temptation and sexual temptation, the desire to go and hang out with my old people. How do I get over it? The Holy Spirit; the Father communicates with me through the Holy Spirit. I am always in the word. God said, "My manifestation is determined by my meditation." I try to stick to that principle. I am thinking about the word all day long. God, you have to manifest yourself so that the darkness around me cannot come in. I am conveying light. The word of God says: "Light has entered into this world..." I have to constantly be in that word. Even now, I cannot be concerned about your perceptions of me. I am not concerned about anyone's perceptions of me. I will walk through the church loud and rambunctious. Why? Because this is my joy. They don't know what I had to battle with ever, let alone yesterday, to even build my faith up because God allowed it.

Simply put, the word of God.

Tell me why you couldn't imagine your life without God.

Everything that I have ever been through has been in the absence of Him. I have seen too much; I have been through too much. I am constantly tempted with the two things that tempted me the most back in the day: sex and drugs. My spiritual warfare was so horrific it manifested itself in the natural realm. The other day, I'm in the city and I am tempted to go to a hotel. I was almost about to submit and the Holy Spirit said, "I love you." I stopped, hugged myself, and said, "I love you too," turned around and went into a Starbucks to go to the bathroom. I am on line and there is a dude in front of me and a dude behind me. The one behind me is walking around in circles because he was on drugs, one familiar spirit. I didn't know anything about the spirit in front me until the dude in the bathroom closed the door. I heard the door click, so it is now in occupied mode. I am still praising God in my mind because I had just overcame the situation with the hotel, then all of a sudden, about 10 minutes passed and the door clicked and it now says vacant. I said I am not going in there, the devil is a liar, I am not going in there. I am not trying to see nothing Father God. I don't know what is going on in that bathroom, that man could be butt-naked – you know the devil is busy. I am not going in that bathroom. I asked the barista to come over and knock on this door because I was positive someone went into the bathroom. She starts asking if they need an ambulance or hospital. The manager comes over, knocks, asking the same questions. They open the door and there was no one in there. There was nobody in there. It was a complete spiritual manifestation. One of my mentors, who is a pastor, said it was a setup for my destruction. If I would've opened that door myself, who knows what would have happened, what could have jumped on me or in me, if I did open the door.

The drug guy was behind me, this thing in front me, and the next day I received my minister's license in the mail. They were trying to stop me from getting to my final destination, which was a dinner with another member of the church. I left Starbucks and was in a state of "Wow, they are coming at me like that? Wow. It is really real."

My eyes are open to the spiritual realm and I couldn't imagine my life without God because now I really know what is out there. I graduated.

If you could describe your relationship with God, what would you say about it? How does it help you day to day?

Intimacy and clarity. I know when I am blatantly being disobedient. We are really close; we are a family. He is really patient with me.

Tell me, what is the most valuable lesson you have learned summed up in one sentence?

Patience is a process of change.

In all my slip-ups, successes, and failures has been patience is a process of change. Love is patience. That is the summation of my salvation. Patience is a process of change.

****

If there was ever a time to join the kingdom of God it is now. There is so much going on around the world, in our country, in our states, townships, municipalities, and homes that we cannot afford to have you wait around much longer. You have read the testimony of this man. You know that there is evil out to get you, to attack you, and to steer you clear away

116

from Jehovah our God and Creator. If you watch the news or even look at your Facebook page, you can see others constantly posting news articles about all of the revolting news that goes on all day long. Personally, it was easier for me not to have a television and not to go on any social media outlets because it was becoming excessive. There has to be a change in this world, and this is the perfect time to heed that calling. You know you are destined for greatness. You know you are a fighter, survivor, and better yet, greater than where you currently are. This year, 2015, is supposed to be a year of promise, new beginnings, and grace. Depending on when you are reading this book, you may have been blessed by the promises of God, you may be running from the promises, or you are still in the waiting phase. Whatever place you are currently in, know that you have to make the Lord Jesus Christ your personal lord and savior in order to understand what that truly means. As the previous testimony proclaims: "Patience is a process of change." You have been patiently waiting for your life to change but you are missing one thing, well two: First, you must make the decision to say yes to making the Lord your savior, and second, you must take the first step to change. Many times people develop a relationship with someone and expect that person to change and adjust to his or her personal standards, but how many times does that actually work out? How many times does the person whom you wish to change actually change? Very few times does this happen because everything ends and begins with YOU! Start a new life today in Christ Jesus, filled with new beginnings and a promise of everlasting life. Say this prayer aloud to openly confess Jesus Christ as your personal lord and savior:

Heavenly Father,

Thank you for this day of life,

Thank you for loving me so much that you sent your son,

Jesus Christ, to die on the cross for my sin.

I believe in my heart that Jesus Christ is the son of God and

On the third day, he rose again.

Today I ask that you come into my life to become my Lord and Savior.

I am born again, I am saved, and I am a new creation.

My best days are ahead of me. Thank you Lord.

I love you, in Jesus' name. Amen.

Welcome to the Kingdom of God!

"For God so loved the world that He gave His only begotten Son, that whoever believes in Him should not perish but have everlasting life."

Please find a Bible-based church and allow God to perform miracles in your life. You will not regret it. These men are living proof of what God is doing and what He has done.

Thank you for reading, and pass this book on to a friend so you can be a blessing in his life.

"That is, that we may be mutually strengthened *and* encouraged *and* comforted by each other's faith, both yours and mine."

Romans 1:12 AMP

God bless you.

www.ingramcontent.com/pod-product-compliance
Lightning Source LLC
Chambersburg PA
CBHW060939040426
42445CB00011B/933